Dedicated to our future leaders: our children!

Author: Zeinab Zaiter Hachem
Illustrator: Vanessa Bueno
Editor: Charlie Kadado (Author & Journalist)

ISBN: 978-1-63821-825-8

The Moon That Shines Bright

On the first day of Ramadan, Nour and Fatima's parents told them a story about how Muslims fast during Ramadan. The girls enjoyed the stories and were eager to ask questions! Their mom and dad were excited to share everything they knew about Ramadan.
The girls wondered if other kids had the same questions. Nour and Fatima's parents assured them that the stories they read during Ramadan will have all the answers.

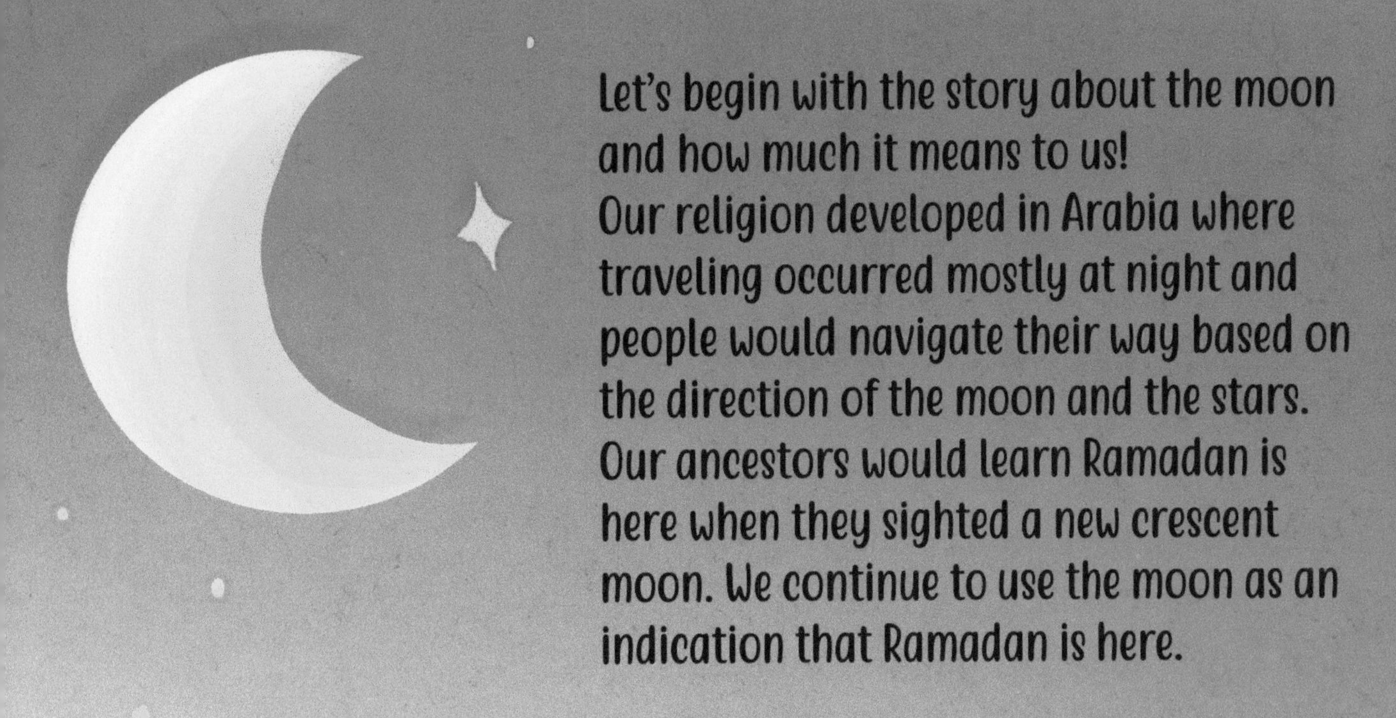

Let's begin with the story about the moon and how much it means to us!
Our religion developed in Arabia where traveling occurred mostly at night and people would navigate their way based on the direction of the moon and the stars.
Our ancestors would learn Ramadan is here when they sighted a new crescent moon. We continue to use the moon as an indication that Ramadan is here.

Suhoor With My Family

It was an exhausting day for Fatima as she had to stay up all night doing homework. Nour loved to sleep, but during the month of Ramadan, she loves to spend that extra time with her family. She made it a habit to get up to help her mom make Suhoor. Suhoor is a breakfast eaten before sunrise during Ramadan. A while later, mom asked Nour to wake up dad and Fatima so that they can eat together before the sun comes up.

Together, they shared a lot of traditional foods, such as yogurt, olives, cheese, and tea. It was their favorite breakfast! What's your favorite breakfast during Ramadan? Fatima and Nour enjoyed having long laughs with their parents and couldn't wait to spend the day helping others. They spent the rest of their Suhoor cleaning up the breakfast table, praying with their parents, and giving each other lots of kisses before going to bed.

A Selfless Day

A man shivered on the ground outside with a sign that says, “Anything helps.” It is so important to develop the habit of giving Sadaqah. Sadaqah is your charitable act toward others, whether it is through your generosity, love, compassion, or faith. Nour and Fatima asked mom if she has extra coins in the car to give to the needy man. Mom reached through the cup holder and found a few quarters. Nour and Fatima insisted on giving the money themselves. They rolled down the window and asked the man to come toward them. They gave the man the change but promised to come back with some food and water.

As the family grabbed their groceries for the day, the girls never stopped thinking about the needy man. Food is so accessible to us that we sometimes forget that it's not in reach for many others. The girls grabbed some extra food and drinks and couldn't wait to meet their friend again. As mom pulled up to the stoplight, the girls gave him the items with smiles from ear to ear. "May God bless you guys always," the man said. Every time they go out, Nour and Fatima started taking extra money with them. Have you started any new habits this Ramadan?

An Empty Stomach

"Uncle Ali, what a beautiful sunny day!" Fatima exclaimed. Uncle Ali invited his nieces for dinner at his house for Iftar. Iftar is the time of day when Muslims break their fast. Iftar happens when the sun sets. Fatima asked her uncle what he was making for the family. "For dinner, we will be having rice with chicken and a side of salad," Ali replied. Fatima suggested that we make a generous amount so that we can give some to a family in need.

Ali knew of a family that could use an extra hand. He called the family and invited them to join us for Iftar. They lightened our home with their companionship! Fatima and Nour spent the evening preparing the table. Iftar approached us fast, and before we knew it, our guests were here! Who is your favorite person to share Iftar with?

Prayers

Fatima wonders how she can get more toys to play with. She says, "Maybe if I had $100, I would be able to buy more toys." She finished her Iftar and went to her room to do Salah. Salah is the prayer that Muslims perform five times per day. Fatima prayed to have more money, but the next morning she didn't get any! She woke up each day hoping the money would show up. When the money never came, she had to think of a different way to earn it.

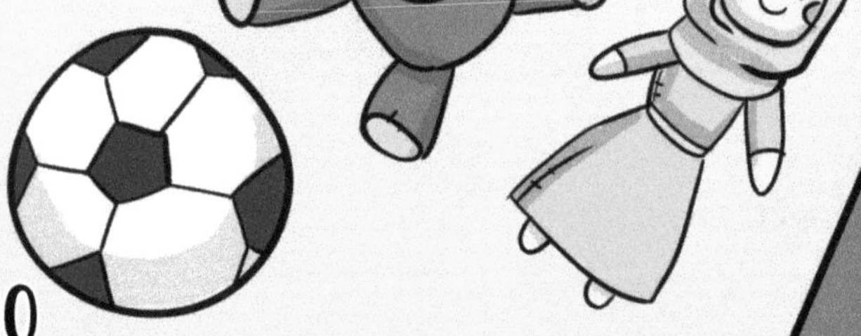

She asked her mom if she can help do housework. The days passed and Fatima earned more than money. She earned responsibilities around the house, such as cleaning her room, cleaning the floor, feeding the birds, and much more. She didn't value money as much and instead thanked God for always guiding her in his own ways.

No One is Watching!

"I will not tell anyone that you drank water. Go ahead and take a sip to break your fast," Manesa told Fatima and Nour. Fatima stood up and replied, "It's not about you telling. God is watching. I wouldn't be happy with myself knowing there are many people around the world dying of thirst, and I broke my fast because I'm a little thirsty." We have this feeling for only one month.

Thankfully, we have the water at our reach while many others do not have that luxury. Fasting is an act of worship to become more compassionate to those in need. Muslims fast from sunrise to sunset during Ramadan. Manesa hugged Fatima and told her that she was right. Fasting teaches us to be more patient and break bad habits.

A Boy Who Lies

Fatima saw her friend Jawad during lunchtime at school and she went to sit with him. Jawad was telling everyone at the table about his long vacation to Florida. Fatima was listening but knew what Jawad was saying was not true because she saw him at tutoring all summer! She didn't want to embarrass Jawad in front of his friends by calling him a liar so she waited until he was done.

Fatima pulled Jawad to the side and asked, "Why were you lying to everyone?" "It makes me cool," Jawad replied. Fatima explained that it is not good behavior to lie and that he should always tell the truth. Real friends love you for being truthful. Jawad agreed with Fatima and promised to always tell the truth. Have you ever made up a story to look or sound cool?

Cheating on a Test

"Psssst! Only one more question," whispered Haidar. Nour was scared to get into trouble with her teacher so she replied, "No! You should have studied!" Before Nour could finish her sentence, her teacher caught her and Haidar. She asked them to stay until everyone left. Nour told the teacher that she was only trying to help Haidar with one question, but he kept asking for more!

Mrs. Rima explained to the kids that it was not okay to cheat because it is untruthful even if it is for one question. She asked Haidar why he didn't study. Haidar replied that he knew Nour would help him.

Mrs. Rima gave both kids a lesson by telling Nour to always say no when someone encourages her to do the wrong thing. Haidar also learned to study next time. Have you ever helped someone when you knew it was the wrong thing to do?

Stealing Money

Dad was getting ready to go to work when Fatima realized that she wanted a dollar to buy a snack at school. Fatima went into her dad's wallet and started digging for cash when Nour caught her! Nour asked Fatima why she was taking money without asking. Fatima replied, "It's only one dollar!" Nour told Fatima that taking anything without asking is called stealing. You should always ask the person you're taking from before you touch their belongings. "It's haram to touch other people's belongings without permission," Nour said.

Haram is the word used to describe something sinful. You should always avoid doing things that are haram so you can be on a good path in life. Fatima apologized to her dad for taking a dollar from his wallet and promised to always ask before doing so. Have you ever taken something without asking?

Standing Up

Ring, ring, ring. "It's time for recess!" the kids exclaimed. Nour and Fatima took turns on the monkey bars. While playing, they noticed Hassan push Batoul off the swing. Fatima shouted, "That's not nice Hassan!" The girls walked up to Hassan and asked him why he pushed Batoul. He replied, "Because I want a turn." Fatima explained to Hassan that he should have asked and waited patiently for a turn. Hassan seemed very sad that his sister Batoul was hurt. He apologized to her and promised that he will be more patient next time. Batoul forgave Hassan and told him that he can use the swing while she played on the monkey bars. Nour was very proud of Fatima for standing up for Batoul. Do you stand up for what's right?

Forgiving Others

Nour couldn't help but remember how easy it was for Batoul to forgive Hassan even though she was hurt. Nour asked Batoul why she forgave Hassan. She explained to Nour that holding on to things for a long time doesn't help. It actually makes you less happy! Nour was surprised but learned a lesson that day.

Earlier, Nour's friend Fatima S. tried apologizing to her. She went to Fatima S. immediately and told her she forgives her for not sharing her toys. Fatima S. was confused but happy. She gave Nour a big hug! Nour told her mom about what happened and said she feels happier when she doesn't let small things bother her. It's very easy to get upset about small things and it takes a big leap to forgive sometimes. Are you still upset at someone and hope to forgive them?

Appreciating Life

"Chirp, chirp," the birds sang. Fatima and Nour woke up to the sounds of the birds begging for food! While the girls were feeding the birds, they noticed one of their birds not feeling well. Fatima rushed to get their dad. He observed one of the birds laying her eggs. The girls were so happy to tell their friends about their bird having babies on the way. Their friends looked at the birds and screamed, "Wow!" Nour told her friends to say "Mashallah" or "Subhan Allah" instead. Mashallah is a word used in Islam to express appreciation, joy, praise, or thankfulness. Nour and Fatima were excited to spend the next couple of weeks making sure nothing happens to the eggs. Subhan Allah means Glory to God and his creations. Will you be saying the word Mashallah and Subhan Allah when you see something beautiful?

Loving One Another

It was a rainy day today. Nour and Fatima love watching the rain but dislike that they can't play with their friends outside. Nour asked her mom if she can invite her friends to play hide and seek inside the house. Mom called Nour and Fatima's friends to ask them to join for a play date. Their friends came within minutes. Fatima told Zahraa to start counting while they hid. When Zahraa found Nour super fast, Nour was very upset and said she did not want to play anymore. She asked Zahraa to go home, but Fatima stopped Nour before she could even finish her sentence. Fatima told Nour it was not nice to treat your friends that way! "It was just a game," Fatima said. Nour apologized to Zahraa and promised to only say kind things in the future. Zahraa forgave Nour and gave her a big hug. Have you ever hurt your friend's feelings and apologized?

Fitting In

It was lunch time at school when Nour spotted her friend Fatme sitting all by herself during lunch. Nour walked up to Fatme and asked her to join her table with the other girls. Fatme said to Nour, "I do not think the girls like me and I'm afraid that they will make fun of me because I'm different than them." Nour assured her that being different makes you beautiful and unique. Fatme insisted on staying by herself but Nour refused and sat with her. Nour explained to Fatme you will always fit in with the right friends as long as you have good Akhlaq. Akhlaq means ethics or morals. When a person has good ethics, they have good values and behavior. They appreciate you for you who are because you are kind, humble, and true to youself. Fatme learned the meaning of fitting in and saw how Nour stayed by her side. Nour has great Akhlaq! Do you surround yourself with friends who have good Akhlaq?

Being Perfect

"The weekend is here!" Nour said with excitement. "Today is the day my mom's friend Zeina comes over!" Although she's their mom's friend, Zeina plays with Nour and Fatima a lot and they have so much fun with her. Nour didn't know what to wear so she tried on so many outfits. She couldn't find the one she liked. She was getting upset with herself when she looked around and noticed her bed was unmade. Nour began to cry and called for her mom.

Her mom came to the room and asked what was wrong. Nour replied, “My room is messy! My toys are everywhere even though I just cleaned up, and I can’t find anything to wear!” Mom replied “Aunt Zeina is not here to see how your room looks or what clothes you’re wearing. She’s here to spend some time with you, and that’s what matters!”. Do you have someone in your life whose visit makes you so happy?

Blaming My Friends

It's practice day at soccer! Nour and Fatima were getting ready for the big game. "It's not fair that Nour always picks who is on her team," Fatima said. "That's why we always lose." Couch Abbas went up to the teams and explained to them that it was important to play as one. The game began with Fatima having the ball. Her friend Malak asked her to pass the ball but Fatima refused and passed it to Eleyna instead. Eleyna went to score and missed the net. The coach gathered the girls and asked them what happened. Fatima blamed Nour for picking better players. She also blamed Malak for distracting her while she was passing the ball. Finally, she blamed Eleyna for not moving fast enough to get closer to the goal!

The coach was disappointed with Nour's answer and explained to the team that we should never blame one another. Coach Abbas explained to the team that if one person makes a mistake, the whole team makes a mistake. We are in the game as one! Nour apologized to everyone and promised to work together with her friends to become a team player. Do you play any sports?

Regretting Mistakes

It was Grandma's birthday. Fatima and Nour forgot to wish their Tata Randa a happy birthday. Tata is an Arabic word for grandma. Tata waited for Nour and Fatima to call her or go visit her home. Nighttime approached and Tata was starting to believe the girls forgot about her big day. Nour and Fatima's mom asked the girls to dress so that they can visit their Tata. The girls asked why they were going during a school night when they could just see her this weekend. Mom told the girls it was their Tata's birthday and she hoped they didn't forget! Nour and Fatima looked at each other in shock. Nour told her mom that she regrets not calling Tata in the morning or buying her a present. Mom explained they should never regret their mistakes because most of the time it makes you appreciate what you have and helps you learn new lessons every day. Can you think of any past mistakes that helped you learn a lesson?

1 2 3 4 5
6 7 8 9 10 11 12
13 14 15 16 17 18 19
20 21 22 23 24 25 26
27 28 29 30

Complaining

"Chicken? Again?" Nour asked her dad. "We just had that food yesterday," Fatima pouted. "At least we're having a warm meal!" dad exclaimed. The girls were watching cartoons on TV when their dad turned it off. He asked them to get dressed to go volunteer with him. They visited an area their dad volunteers in almost every weekend! When the kids saw paper and waste all over the ground, they did not look too happy. They began to question the reason their dad brought them there. Their dad handed them some gloves and asked them to hand out food to needy people.

After the girls served hundreds of people, their dad handed them garbage bags and asked the girls to pick up the litter on the ground. The girls finished their volunteer work and asked their dad, with tears in their eyes, if they can come help out every weekend. The girls apologized to dad for complaining about their food and promised to always appreciate what they have. What are your blessings in life?

As-Salaam-Alaykum

Grandpa Hussein came to visit Nour and Fatima with his nephews Ameer, Karam, and Mustapha. Fatima ran downstairs and welcomed her cousins and grandpa. “What’s up guys?” she asked. Their cousins responded with the same wording. Grandpa Hussein was sad to hear the kids welcome each other that way. He sat them down to show them a better way of welcoming one another. He told the kids to always use the word, “As-Salaam-Alaykum” when greeting each other. The kids asked Grandpa Hussein what it meant.

He said, “As-Salaam-Alaykum” is a greeting in Arabic that means peace be upon you. It is used when greeting our friends, family, brothers, and sisters in faith.” Grandpa explained that when they say “As-Salaam-Alaykum” to someone, they are also greeting the angels that sit on their shoulders and record their good and bad deeds. The kids thanked their grandpa and promised to do their best to use it from now on. How do you greet everyone?

Confidence

Mona was taking Nour and Fatima shopping and they couldn't wait to see her! Nour and Fatima got dressed as fast as possible and waited for Mona to pick them up. On their way to the mall, Fatima asked Nour if she was ready to buy her Eid dress. "I'm not sure I will look good in the dress," Nour replied. "I think I look fat in all of the dresses. I would rather buy jeans and a hoodie." Fatima told Nour that she looks amazing the way she is. "You don't know how it feels," Nour shrugged. In the store, Fatima and Mona placed a few dresses in the cart.

Mona tried on a few dresses in front of Nour and Fatima. "Do they look good on me?" she asked. "Amazing!" Nour and Fatima replied in unison. "I think it looks horrible on me! I don't look good in anything," Mona replied. Nour was shocked and asked Mona why she said that. After all, the dresses looked beautiful on her! Mona explained to Nour that she was acting the same way Nour was when everyone told her she looked amazing no matter what she wore. Nour learned that the way you look on the inside matters more than the way you look on the outside. You should always know you look amazing no matter what shape, size, or color you are. Are you confident with yourself?

Favorite Part of the Day

Nour and Fatima went for a walk with mom to get to know their neighbors. One of their neighbors waved her hand to the girls but was unable to walk. Fatima and Nour walked up to the neighbor to talk with her. They found out that she had a cat named Lilo. Lilo was a beautiful Persian cat with blue eyes. The girls finished their walk and headed back home to make Iftar. After dinner, the family laid out their prayer rugs to pray Laylatul Qadr.

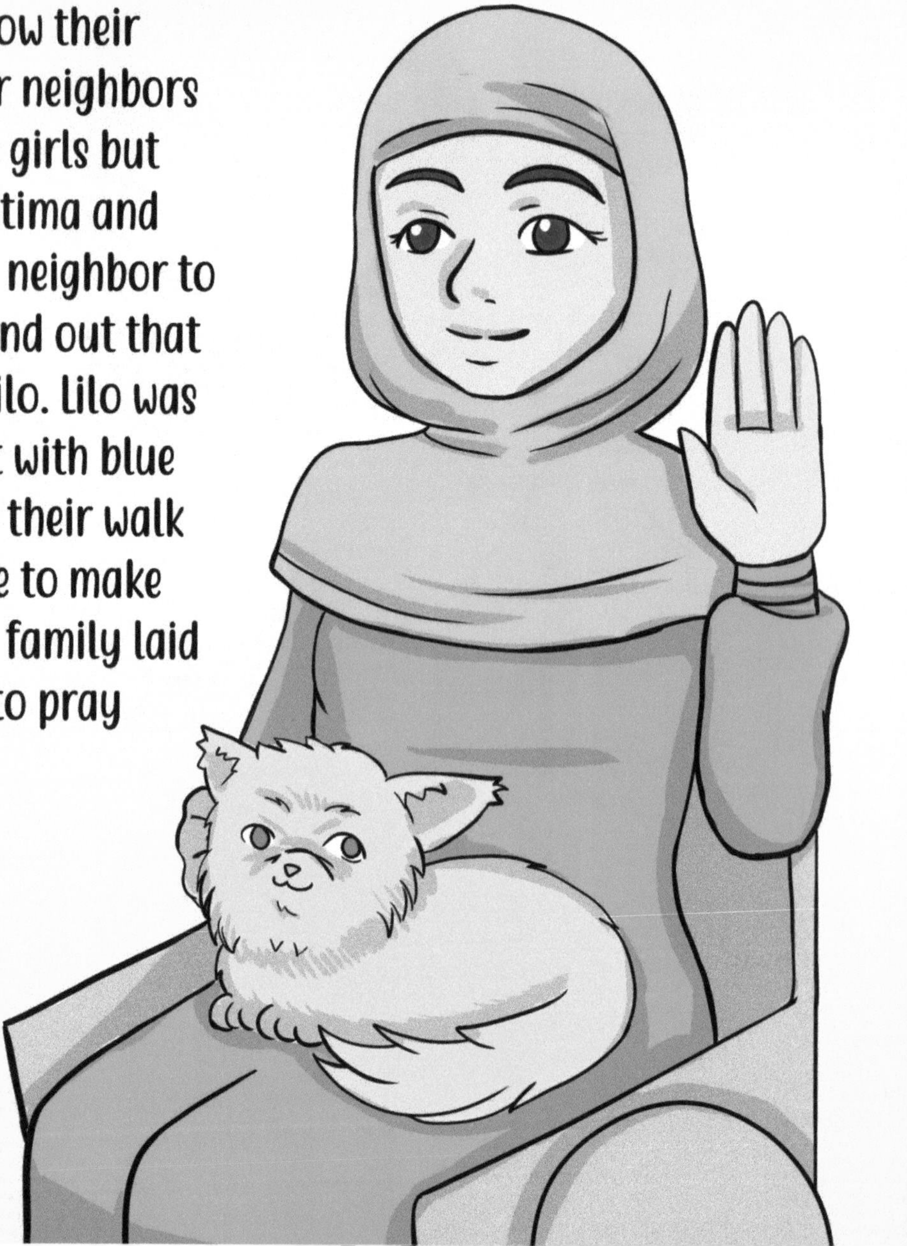

Laylatul Qadr is the most important prayer performed during Ramadan. Praying Laylatul Qadr out of faith and sincerity shall have all their past sins forgiven. Nour and Fatima wanted to take this day to pray for their neighbor who couldn't walk. They prayed for her faith to always be strong and happy. What are some things that you pray for?

Bismillah

There was a big test the next day and Fatima was super nervous about it. Fatima was so nervous that she couldn't eat breakfast. The girls were waiting patiently for the teacher to pass the test to everyone in the class. Fatima began to cry. Mr. Joseph asked Fatima why she was so upset. Fatima replied that she was super nervous before the test and didn't know how to overcome her fear. Mr. Joseph assured her that she always does great on her test. "You can always say Bismillah," Mr. Joseph said. Bismillah means in the name of Allah. It is used to remove fear from a person and gives them a feeling of comfort. Fatima felt a little more relaxed when she spoke to her teacher. "I love learning," Fatima told Mr. Joseph. She began to practice the habit of saying Bismillah and relaxing before taking a test. Soon, she noticed her nervous behavior go away! What's your favorite subject in school?

Inviting My Family Over

It was the final 10 days of Ramadan and the girls wanted to spend time with their family to learn more about becoming better people. The girls decided that it was a good idea to have all their cousins over for Iftar. They prepared grape leaves, salad, fries, lentil soup, and dates. Dates are very important in Ramadan since Prophet Mohamed used to advise people to eat them while breaking their fast. The girls ate their Iftar, washed the dishes, and sat down to talk. The girls talked about Ramadan and what other good deeds they can do to help others.

Their cousin Leya said, "Maybe we should pray for the poor tonight." "That's a great idea!" Nour said. The girls went to the bathroom one by one for Wudu. Wudu is an Islamic procedure to cleanse parts of the body for purification. Wudu is an important part of ritual purification in Islam. The girls spent the rest of the night praying for the poor, vulnerable, homeless, and the countries facing war. It was a blessed night filled with love and giving. How do you spend your last 10 days of Ramadan?

Everything Happens for a Reason

Nour was ready to head to her cousin Emma's house. Today is Emma's birthday and Nour didn't want to be late. Nour looked at the clock and noticed that it was almost two in the afternoon. She's going to be late! She tried to hurry and wrap the present as fast as she could. She didn't know why she overlooked the time. "I should've wrapped the present the day before," Nour told her mom. On their way to Emma's house, Nour noticed a lot of traffic at the light. She asked her mom why there was so much traffic. Mom said, "There is a huge car accident ahead. It's okay to be late." Nour remembered a saying her dad always tells her. "Aasa an takrahoo shayan wahuwa khayrun lakum," he says. It means, perhaps you hate something but it is good for you. Has anything happened to you that made you upset, but something better happened later?

Friday

What is your favorite day of the week? Why do you enjoy it? Nour and Fatima's favorite day of the week is Friday. Friday is very important for Muslims because it is a sacred day. Muslims believe that God chose this day as a dedicated day of worship. It is the day the first human, Adam, was created. Fatima and Nour love when the family gets together at the Mosque to pray with their friends and family. Fatima enjoys spending the day with her Tata Zeinab reading the Quran. Fatima enjoys listening to her Tata reading the Quran. If Fatima doesn't understand certain verses, her Tata translates it for her. Where do you pray on Friday?

Making Dua

Dua is when Muslims from all over connect with God and ask him for forgiveness, guidance, and favors. Dua is also used to thank God for what he provided. The girls' uncle Ali always reminds them to say these two Duas everyday.
Dua to say when waking up:

اَلْحَمْدُ لِلَّهِ الَّذِي عَافَانِي فِي جَسَدِي، وَرَدَّ عَلَيَّ رُوحِي، وَأَذِنَ لِي بِذِكْرِهِ

All praise is for Allah who gave us life after having taken it from us and unto Him is the resurrection.
Dua to say after eating a meal:

الْحَمْدُ لِلَّهِ الَّذِي أَطْعَمَنَا وَسَقَانَا وَجَعَلَنَا مِنَ الْمُسْلِمِينَ

Praise be to Allah who has fed us and given us drink and made us Muslims.

Habits That Stick

"The journey this Ramadan has been a blessing," Fatima told her mom. "I learned so much more this year." Mom replied, "I hope you learned how to devote yourself more this year." Nour was so happy that she spent Ramadan with the people she loves. With her pencil and notebook in hand, she sat down to write every good habit she learned this Ramadan. She wanted to continue becoming a better version of herself by providing more love every day. What is something kind you have done this Ramadan?

Baking for Eid

Today is such a special day. Fatima and Nour have a special tradition in the family where they visit Tata Zeinab's and Jido Mohamed's house to make Ka'ak. They also put all of the Sadaqa in envelopes to give to the needy. Nour and Fatima start their day by washing their hands and helping Tata mix all the ingredients together. It's so much fun cooking with her since she lets them choose the shapes of Ka'ak they want. Ka'ak is an Arabic word for biscuit, and it is sometimes stuffed with dates.

Once they are done making Ka'ak, they join Jido in the living room. This is one of their favorite traditions with Jido. He opens the Sadaqah boxes and has them place money in each envelope for people in need. Sadaqah means voluntary charity and it's very important in Islam. What's a special tradition you have in your family?

Getting Ready for Eid

Nour and Fatima are up and ready to start their day. The girls get their cookie bags out and start to place some Ka'ak in each bag. They then head over to their neighbors' homes to give them out. Their neighbors are overjoyed to taste the best Ka'ak around. Fatima and Nour head back home to help mom clean the house. They need to prepare for visitors tomorrow. Fatima and Nour place their Eid clothes out for ironing and take out their sparkly shoes. Nour can't wait to see the whole family tomorrow. Fatima is a bit sad that Ramadan has come to an end but is thankful it has taught her so much. Are you ready for Eid tomorrow?

Eid is Here

Mom woke up early to get the girls' clothing ready. It was time to head to the mosque for Eid prayer. Eid is a worldwide festival and celebration for Muslims. It is a festival to break the fast at the end of the holy month of Ramadan. Nour and Fatima woke up and put on their Eid clothes. After praying, they visited all of their grandparents, uncles, aunts, cousins, friends, and neighbors. It was one of the happiest days of the year, especially when it reminds you of everything God has blessed us with. What did you do this Eid?

CPSIA information can be obtained
at www.ICGtesting.com
Printed in the USA
LVHW070942080321
680862LV00019B/191

9 781638 218258